PESKY

KINGFISHER
An imprint of Larousse plc
Elsley House,
24-30 Great Titchfield Street,
London, W1P 7AD

First published by Larousse plc 1996

Copyright © Larousse plc and © D. C. Thomson & Co. Ltd 1996.
Factual material and non-character illustration © Larousse plc
1996. Comic character illustration © D. C. Thomson & Co. Ltd
1996. The Beano title and logo is the property of
D. C. Thomson & Co. Ltd.

All rights reserved.

A CIP catalogue record for this book is available from the
British Library

ISBN 0 7534 0080 4

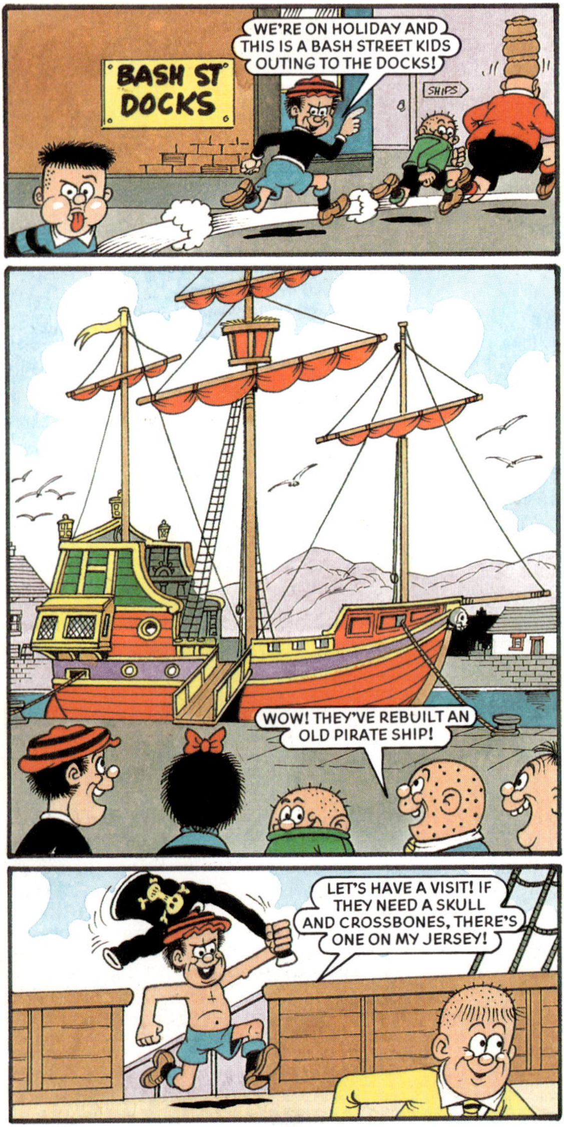

WHAT IS A PIRATE?

Pirates have existed for as long as man has sailed the oceans carrying cargo of value. The word 'pirate' comes from an old Greek word meaning 'sea-going robber'. Many of the first pirates were escaped prisoners or slaves or men on the run from the navy. Others were simply people who wanted a life of freedom and excitement on the high seas!

EARLY PIRATES

As long ago as the 7th century BC pirates sailed the Mediterranean Sea. The merchant ships of great early civilizations such as the Greeks, Romans and Phoenicians were often attacked, and their cargoes of precious metals stolen.

HIDE AND SEEK

Early pirates did not always have to venture out into open waters. Merchant ships on the Mediterranean tended to sail close to the coastline. All the pirates had to do was wait in a sheltered inlet for passing trade ships, and then sail out to attack them!

All sorts of strange people became pirates!

A pirate ship of the 1500s following a galleon.

HOW TO GET STARTED AS A PIRATE

1 Develop a pirate personality. (Nasty, smelly, cruel and greedy.)

2 Find a ship to sail in. (A reasonably big ship is best.)

3 Find a ship carrying lots of treasure you can attack. (Make sure the ship is carrying treasure and not tonnes of horse manure or shellfish, or something else equally difficult to sell or trade.)

4 Find a place to hide after you've attacked. (Not under your bed – it's the first place most people will look for you.)

THROW THE CAPTIVE BACK. HE'S HORRIBLE!

I'M WORTH MORE THAN THAT!

One of the most famous people to be captured by pirates was Julius Caesar. He was 'kidnapped' in 78 BC and held to ransom by his captors. The pirates demanded 25 silver pieces for the safe return of Julius. However, Caesar felt that his captors were not asking for enough ransom money. He told them that he was worth at least 50 silver pieces! He was released after six weeks, when the money was paid. Later, he led an army to hunt down and kill his captors.

PIRATES OF THE NORTH

For hundreds of years, the Vikings or coastal tribes of Scandinavia survived by raiding other villages and robbing passing ships. In the 9th century, the Vikings began to steal from ships on the open seas. The word 'Viking' means 'going on an overseas raid'.

OUT FOR GLORY

Vikings were fierce warriors who believed that glory in battle meant everything. They were known to catch spears in mid-flight and hurl them back at their opponents!

The Vikings attacked ships and raided the coastlines of Britain, Ireland, France, Russia and North Africa.

HERE WE COME!

The sight of a Viking ship on the horizon was enough to terrify people. The Vikings were expert shipbuilders and navigators. They steered using the sun and the stars as guides, while their strong but light longboats allowed them to sail great distances across the open seas. Each longboat was powered by oars and a single sail made of wool.

Viking longboats landing.

A longboat

VIKING WEAPONS

The Vikings excelled as pirates. On land they attacked with broadswords, spears or big axes. But when they were fighting at sea, they preferred a small, light axe.

FRIGHTENING FACES

Raiding parties of up to 100 Vikings were carried in the longboats. To frighten their opponents, they decorated their boats with shields and fearsome figureheads.

A VIKING LONGBOAT

The maximum length of a Viking longboat was 46 m. It could travel at a speed of 10 knots. The ships were usually rowed by Viking warriors who were famous for their terrifying strength.

HALL OF FAME

Erik the Red (950-1010) was one of the fiercest Norsemen of all. He is most famous for discovering Greenland.

Viking warriors were well armed.

THE CORSAIRS

At the end of the 11th century, wars broke out between Christian Europe and Islamic nations in the Middle East and North Africa. Europe thought they would lose control of the Mediterranean, so they decided to enlist the help of pirates. But Islam had its pirates too! Christian and Muslim pirates who helped their countries were known as 'Corsairs'.

HAND OVER THE BOOTY!

The wars between the Christians and the Muslims went on for hundreds of years. During this time, Corsairs were encouraged to attack as many enemy ships as possible. As long as they promised to give a generous share of the booty to their military leaders, they were allowed to live the life of a pirate.

An Algerian Corsair.

SHIP-SHAPE

Corsairs sailed in ships called galleys. Muslim galleys were 55 m long and 5 m wide. The oars they used were 4.5 m long and it took six men to row each one. These galleys could easily sail as fast as 16 kmph over short distances. Christian galleys usually had more cannons and they often had two or three masts instead of one.

A Christian galley.

The Barbarossa brothers.

LIFE AT SEA

The Corsairs' needed slaves to row their galleys. Slaves were treated badly, and they did not live long. They had to row night and day with only bread and water to eat and drink. They were often beaten and as soon as they died, they were replaced by newly captured slaves.

THE LAST BATTLE

The Battle of Lapanto in 1571 was the Corsairs' last great battle. At least 500 Muslim ships were hit and 20,000 pirates were either killed or captured.

FEARSOME BROTHERS

The two most famous Muslim pirates were the Barbarossa brothers, Aruj and Kheir-ed-Din. They were known to be very cruel and were feared by their enemies. They probably seemed even more frightening as they both had long red beards.

THE SPANISH MAIN

When Christopher Columbus sailed from Spain in 1492, he was looking for a new trade route to India. Instead of finding this, he found America! As soon as he returned to Spain, his king and queen laid claim to the waters surrounding the southeast of the continent. This area soon became known as the 'Spanish Main'.

GALLEONS OF GOLD

From about 1500 onwards, the Spanish navy plundered the area around the Caribbean and Gulf of Mexico of its gold and precious stones. This treasure was loaded on great galleons and shipped back across the Atlantic to Spain. Almost immediately the ships were attacked by pirates from England and France. For although the galleons were very well armed, they were slow and difficult to steer. This made them easy targets for the fast pirate ships.

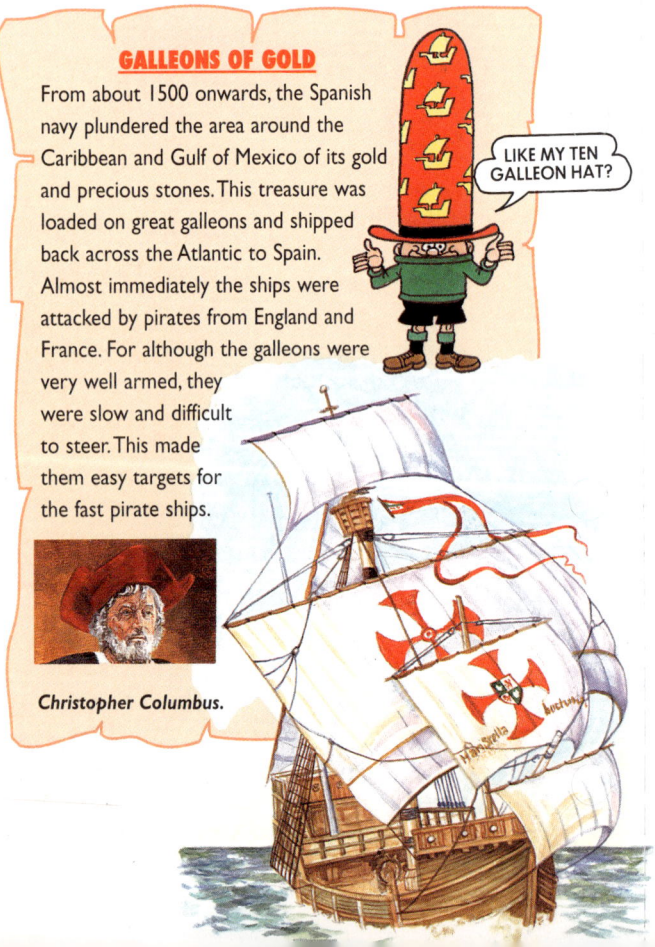

LIKE MY TEN GALLEON HAT?

Christopher Columbus.

MAKING MONEY

The Spanish began mining for gold and silver in Mexico using the Indians as slave labour. Doubloons were the highest value gold coins. Galleons laden with doubloons sailed back across the Atlantic.

VALUABLE PRISONERS

Spanish conquistadors captured a number of native South American kings. They demanded huge ransoms of gold for their release.

A South American king.

AZTEC GOLD

In 1519, the Spanish explorer Hernan Cortez landed with an army in Mexico. He found a country rich in precious metals. Mexico was inhabited by ancient peoples including the Aztecs. Their civilizations did not survive the Spanish invasions.

Cortez plunders the Aztecs.

I'VE FOUND AMERICA!

WHO LOST IT?

The term *Spanish Main* originally meant the parts of the American mainland extending from Mexico to Peru. It later included the Caribbean as well.

THE PRIVATEERS

Countries such as England, France and Portugal weren't at all happy that Spain was becoming so rich. These countries commissioned their best 'private' seamen to steal as much Spanish treasure as they could.

DON'T LOOK. THESE ARE PRIVATE EARS!

SAFETY IN NUMBERS

Privateers sailed to the Americas and they too began loading their ships with valuable cargo. But they didn't just stop there. Whenever possible, they attacked Spanish galleons. When forced to defend themselves, the Spanish tended to fight as if they were on land. They would board the attacking vessel and then fight in hand-to-hand combat. Eventually, Spanish treasure ships were forced to sail in fleets in order to protect themselves and their cargo.

PIRATE FOR HIRE

During the 1500s thousands of privateers sailed across the Atlantic Ocean in search of Spanish galleons. While they gave most of the booty they captured to the government who provided their ships and crew, most privateers also managed to become very rich in their own right.

SNEAKY ATTACK!

The best time to attack a galleon was when it had just begun its voyage. Galleons relied on strong winds to power their massive sails, and it often took some time before they found a favourable wind. So one pirate tactic was to wait in a sheltered bay nearby, ready to attack.

LOST TREASURES

Sometimes the Spanish melted down the solid gold jewellery that they plundered from the Aztecs and the Incas because it would take up less space in the ship's hold.

A treasure chest

PEGLEG

One of France's most famous privateers was a man called François le Clerk. He had a wooden leg and was nicknamed Pie de Palo – 'Pegleg'.

SO THAT'S WHERE PIRATES GET WOODEN LEGS FROM!

Pirates, flying the skull and crossbones flag, attacking a galleon.

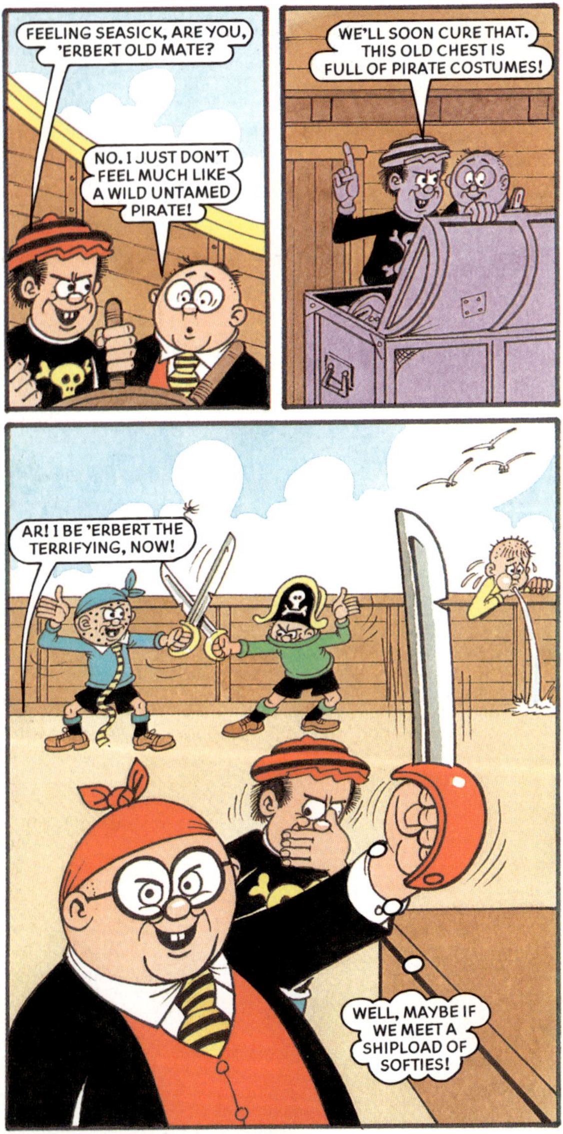

A SPANISH GALLEON

Spanish galleons were big, powerful ships. While many were attacked by pirates, many more sailed unharmed back to Spain with their cargoes intact. They usually had a crew of at least 200 men and carried up to 60 cannons. When smaller and swifter pirate vessels started attacking them, the Spanish began to sail in convoys of up to 100 ships.

The hull of a galleon floated high in the water. This enabled loading to take place in shallow bays and rivers.

Because Spanish galleons carried lots of cannons, pirate ships tried to avoid direct confrontation. Instead, pirates would try to shoot the crew using muskets.

The maximum length of a galleon was 43 m.

One of the most important jobs on a Spanish galleon was held by the man in the crow's nest. His job was to look out for pirates.

PRIVATEERS DRAKE AND HAWKINS

Francis Drake and his cousin John Hawkins were among the most famous English privateers. Drake went to sea at the age of 14, and by the time he was 20 he had his own ship. His successes encouraged many other English adventurers.

I'M SIR FRANCIS DUCK!

TREASURE TROVE

Drake began his career accompanying his cousin John Hawkins, who sold slaves to the Spanish plantations in the Caribbean. Hawkins moved on to plundering Spanish galleons. Not to be outdone, in 1572 Drake raided the treasure port of Nombre de Dios. He stole enough treasure to build 30 warships.

MULE TRAINS

Drake did not always set out to capture Spanish galleons. At one point he resorted to capturing mule trains carrying gold to Spanish ports. He was hated and feared by the Spanish, and his activities brought England and Spain to the point of war.

Sir Francis Drake

BIGGER SHIPS

Early privateers sailed in small ships with crews of about 40 men. Later they used large merchant ships. The merchant ships could carry many more men as well as lots more stolen treasure!

Elizabeth I

The Spanish Armada in battle.

THE NEW WORLD

In 1585-1586, Francis Drake sailed across the Atlantic to raid the Spanish colonies in the New World. This was one of his most famous voyages, and became known as his 'Descent on the Indies'.

DRAKE'S DRUM

Drake carried a drum on board ship on all of his many voyages. It was probably beaten when Drake was about to attack a Spanish galleon. The drum still exists, and some people believe that it will sound a frightening warning beat if ever England is in danger!

LOCAL HERO

Drake's adventures as a privateer and his successful defence of England against the Spanish Armada in 1588 made him a national hero. Queen Elizabeth I made him a knight and gave him a beautiful sword.

HERE COME THE BUCCANEERS

YOU'RE NOT EATING ME!

The story of the buccaneers begins when many runaway slaves, criminals and European settlers went to live on the island of Hispaniola in the 16th and 17th centuries. When these settlers sold food to passing pirate ships, the Spanish became very angry. They sent galleons to attack the island and drive the settlers out. Many of the people fled to live a pirate's life on the island of Tortuga.

WHERE DID YOU GET THAT NAME?

While living on Hispaniola, the local Indians or Arawaks introduced the settlers to a diet of barbecued pig – or 'boucan'. They taught the settlers how to cook the meat in smokehouses. This was one of the foods the settlers sold to passing pirate ships, so they became known as 'boucaniers', or buccaneers.

SNEAKY PIRATES

When buccaneers first began attacking merchant ships they used hollow tree trunks as boats. Later they crept up on the galleons in small boats called *pinnaces*. A handful of men could take control of large galleons before the merchant sailors even knew what was happening.

A small buccaneer boat creeping up on a large galleon.

TIME FOR A BATH

Buccaneers often dressed in animal hide, and were usually very smelly and bloody. Their most hated enemy was the Spanish.

MOVING HOME

As the buccaneers grew in number they moved to Jamaica. Britain didn't mind the buccaneers joining them on the island as they knew they would help to keep the Spanish away.

PIRATE LAW

Buccaneers were perhaps the wildest pirates of all. However, buccaneer groups had their own laws, and their leaders were often very severe. One famous buccaneer leader was Henry Morgan, whose group was known as the 'Brethren of the Coast'. His attacks on the Spanish were approved by the British, and he later became governor of Jamaica.

COSTING AN ARM AND A LEG

Buccaneers had a strange insurance policy. A man who lost his right hand was given 600 pieces of eight. If he lost his left arm, he got 500. (Pieces of eight were large coins, so-called because each was worth eight small coins.)

Buccaneer insurance policy.

A PIG'S BREAKFAST!

The buccaneer Rock Braziliano once roasted two Spaniards when they refused to give him their pigs for food.

FRIGHTFUL FLAGS

Pirate flags were fierce and cruel-looking. Many pirates flew their own flags, hoping that their terrifying designs would make ships give in without a fight.

Jack Rackham *Thomas Tew*

THE JOLLY ROGER

Some pirates flew a red flag to warn their enemies that they would be treated without mercy if they tried to resist. The French called the red flag the 'Joli Rouge' which means pretty red. It is thought that British sailors took this name and turned it into Jolly Roger. But another story tells of a Tamil pirate from southern India, called Ali Raja. When he sailed the waters, he flew a red flag too. English sailors called his red flag, 'Ally Roger's' flag. But it wasn't long before all pirate flags became known as the Jolly Roger.

SKULL AND CROSSBONES

This was the most famous pirate flag of all. It is thought that pirates took the design from the ship's log (a kind of ship's diary), where it represented a death on board.

PIRATE ATTACK!

Pirates looked mean and nasty, but they'd avoid a fight if they could. Their motto was 'always live to fight another day'. To make sure of their own survival, they never attacked a heavily armed ship. Instead, they picked on weak or slow ships. Even then they flew fake flags as they approached, or disguised themselves as women!

Pirates giving a ship a 'broadside' – a blast from their cannons.

DREADFUL DIN

Most pirate ships had a kind of orchestra on board. On the count of three these musicians created the most appalling din with drums and wind instruments, while the pirates danced, waved cutlasses and yelled blood-curdling threats. If for some peculiar reason this didn't persuade the ship under threat to surrender, then the pirates drew along side it and boarded it.

PIRATE WEAPONS

Pirates used a wide range of weapons most effectively:

matchlock

The Musket
A musket was a long-range gun. Pirates opened fire with muskets as they approached enemy ships. It was too clumsy to use when boarding a ship for hand-to-hand combat.

Three iron discs
These were sharpened discs of iron attached to cords. Pirates whirled them over their heads. They could kill or seriously maim a person with them.

Grappling irons
Grappling irons were hooks used for pulling ships together.

Cutlass
A cutlass was a curved short sword ideal for combat at close quarters.

Blunderbuss
The blunderbuss was a scatter gun filled with lead shot – or whatever else was handy. It was most effective when firing into crowds of sailors on deck.

Flintlock pistol
A flintlock was a gun's firing mechanism. A spark struck from the flint set light to the pistol's gunpowder, and the bullet was fired.

Boarding axe
This was used to smash down doors. (Pirates didn't like to waste time when it came to finding treasure!)

Short dagger
A weapon perfect for hand-to-hand fighting.

TREASURE CHESTS

Pirates would steal anything, even if it was nailed down! A medicine chest was considered very valuable, as pirates tended to be an unhealthy lot. But coins such as ducats, doubloons, shillings and guineas were what pirates wanted most. If they made off with valuable objects such as jewels, they would have to trade them for cash once they reached port.

A WELL-PAID JOB

In 1693 the famous American pirate Thomas Tew captured a rich ship in the Indian Ocean. Every member of the crew received a share of the booty worth about 3,000 pounds. In today's money, their share would have made them all millionaires!

THE GOLDEN MAST

Some pirates became so wealthy that one known pirate, Kapitan Stortebeker, had a ship with a golden mast.

HATS OFF, LADS!

In 1769, some English pirates were hanged for robbing a Dutch ship of 60 hats.

HIT AND RUN

Speed was always the pirate's most important weapon. The tactic of 'hit and run' was the best way to capture cargo ships.

Burying treasure

CAPTAIN JACK'S PIRATE QUIZ 1

Now all you 'land lubbers', let's see how you fare with a pirate quiz! If you don't score full pirate marks, Captain Jack might just have yer toes for breakfast! (Watch out for the special trick questions!)

WHAT'S WRONG WITH THIS PICTURE?

1. Who was captured by pirates in 78BC?

2. Which pirate wears the biggest hat?

3. What is a Viking boat called?

4. Where does a pirate keep his booty?

5. Who were the two most famous Muslim pirates?

6. Where do sick pirate ships go?

7. When did Christopher Columbus sail to America?

8. What lies at the bottom of the sea and shivers?

9. Which Spanish explorer arrived in Mexico in 1519?

10. What floats in the sea shouting 'knickers'?

11. Why did pirates attack ships at the start of a voyage?

12. How did the buccaneers get their name?

13. How do you stop a pirate biting his nails?

14. What did pirates use a boarding axe for?

15. What goes "Ha, ha, Jim lad, 'thud'?

16. What kind of booty did pirates most like to find?

WHO WAS THE UGLIEST FIGUREHEAD?

ANSWERS

1. Julius Caesar. 2. The one with the biggest head. 3. A longboat. 4. At the end of his leggy. 5. The Barbarossa brothers, Aruj and Kheir-ed-Din. 6. To the dock. 7. 1492. 8. A nervous wreck. 9. Hernan Cortez. 10. Crude oil 11. Because it could take some time before a ship found a favourable, or strong wind to power its large sails. Until it did, it couldn't move very fast. 12. They were called buccaneers because of the smoked bacon or 'boucan' they cooked and sold to pirates. 13. Chop his fingers off. 14. To smash down doors. 15. A pirate with a wooden leg. 16. Coins such as ducats, doubloons, shillings and guineas.

29

LIFE ONBOARD A PIRATE SHIP

As long as you didn't mind the smell, terrible diet, bad manners and long hours, then being on a pirate ship wasn't all that bad. Pirate ships stank of sea-sodden clothes and stagnant water called bilge. And they didn't have toilets. Instead, pirates had to squat over a hole called 'the head' in the bow of the ship!

I'M BORED
Pirates could spend several weeks at sea before they found a likely treasure ship to plunder. During this time the crew could become very bored. The captain had to be able to control his crew by making them fear and respect him. But often the crew were asked to vote on which course they thought the ship should take.

Hauling ropes

KEEPING CLEAN
Pirates hardly ever changed their clothes and apart from jumping into the ocean from time to time, they never washed.

The pirate's captain had to answer to his crew.

YOU'RE OUT!
Pirates had their own rules. If their captain wasn't making them rich enough, he might simply be thrown overboard!

SICK AT SEA

Because living conditions on board were so awful, pirates were often ill. They suffered from malaria, yellow fever and typhus. An infection called gangrene often spread in flesh wounds and the victim would have to have the limb amputated.

Oranges could prevent scurvy.

A SCURVY LOT

Many pirates suffered from a disease called scurvy – the result of an unhealthy diet, that caused bleeding gums, bad breath and, sometimes, death. The only way of preventing scurvy was a diet of fresh fruit. But this was often harder to find at sea than a treasure chest.

DIRTY PASSENGERS

Every pirate ship had a population of rats. As well as being disease carriers, they gnawed their way through just about everything, including the ship's hull!

A rat

ALL TOGETHER

After a battle or storm, the pirate crew were responsible for repairing their ship. They would have to mend sails and damaged timbers.

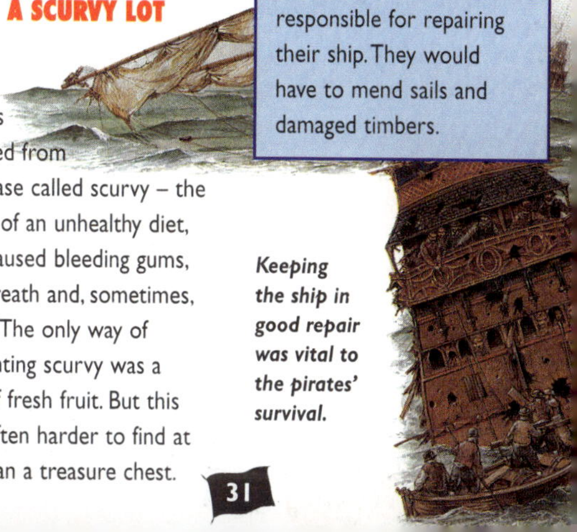

Keeping the ship in good repair was vital to the pirates' survival.

PIRATE CODE OF CONDUCT

Before joining a pirate ship, men had to swear to obey the rules of conduct. It was important for the captain to keep his ship under control – especially since the men were often outlaws and criminals. The rules tended to be the same on every pirate ship. Pirates had to swear on a bible or an axe that they would obey them on pain of death.

1 Every man shall obey civil command.

2 The captain will receive one and a half share in all 'prizes'.

3 The master, carpenter, boatswain and gunner will receive one and a quarter share in all 'prizes'.

4 Men caught stealing will have their noses slit, or at the captain's discretion, be marooned.

5 Anyone caught trying to run away will be marooned.

6 Any man caught striking another will receive 39 lashes.

7 All lights and candles to be out by 8 o'clock.

8 Musicians will play every day except Sunday.

PIRATE FOOD

I'M TRYING TO CATCH A FLYING FISH!

'Food' is perhaps the wrong word to describe a pirate's diet. Their meals were so disgusting that they drank up to a gallon of alcohol a day just to forget them. The only meat they had was 'cured' – smoked until it was as tough as old boots!

TURTLE FOR DINNER

Whenever they could, pirates caught and ate turtles. Turtles were usually the only kind of fresh meat they could get their hands on. Pirates also quite liked to eat soft-shelled turtle eggs.

BIRD STEW

If pirates caught a bird they would put the entire creature into a pot – with peppers, if they had some – and simmer it until the bird was nice and mushy. Yum Yum!

CACKLE FRUIT

In the 17th and 18th centuries, pirate ships carried hens to provide both eggs and meat. Pirates called eggs 'cackle fruit'.

WORMY BISCUITS

Ships' biscuits called 'hard tack' were part of a pirate's daily diet. They were made from flour and water and were often so full of worms and weevils that pirates ate them at night so they couldn't see them wriggling about!

DRINK UP

On board ship, it was difficult to preserve fresh water. Beer was the preferred drink, and pirate ships carried hundreds of barrels of it.

33

PIRATE PUNISHMENTS

Life on board a pirate ship was tough. If a pirate disobeyed a command he could be severely punished. Two of the most serious crimes a pirate could commit were to fall asleep while on watch, or to be a coward in battle. As these acts were considered dangerous to the welfare of fellow pirates, they usually cost the sleepy or cowardly pirate his life.

YOUR TIME'S UP!

The death penalty could be carried out in several ways. The condemned man could be shot or forced to 'walk the plank' until he fell into the sea. Or he was taken up into the rigging and pushed off so that he fell on to the deck below.

Walking the plank

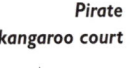

Pirate kangaroo court

"I WON'T DO IT AGAIN!"

Sometimes punishment was intended to make a pirate think again before committing a crime. If a pirate threatened an officer, he could have his hand chopped off. If he stole from a fellow pirate, he could have his ears and nose slit.

TERRIBLE TORTURES

A pirate's punishment depended upon the severity of his offence. His shipmates had many ingenious methods of tormenting him. These included:

Keel-hauling
The pirate was tied to the back of the ship by a piece of rope and dragged through the water.

Sweating
A circle of candles was placed around the mast. The pirate was forced to crawl around the circle of candles, prodded by sharp knives, until he collapsed with exhaustion.

Flogging
The culprit was whipped, usually with a 'cat-o'-nine tails'.

Tar and feathers
The culprit was smothered in hot, burning tar and hundreds of feathers.

Marooning
Pirates who tried to run away were left on a desert island with a bottle of water, a gun and some ammunition. This was as good as a death sentence.

Flogging

PIRATE WOMEN

Women were not usually allowed on board a naval or pirate ship. It was thought to be unlucky. Nevertheless, there were several exceptional women who dared to live the life of a pirate. Many wore mens' clothes, and tales of their great adventures show that they were just as brave as their male companions.

IT WAS UNLUCKY TO BE ON MINNIE'S PIRATE SHIP!

COBHAM THE CRUEL

Maria Cobham was one of the meanest female pirates of all. She was known to put prisoners in sacks and throw them overboard, and she often used her officers as target practice. Her husband was a pirate too. By the time they retired from a life on the high seas they were very rich.

DRAGON OF THE SEAS

Ching Yih Saou was a ferocious Chinese pirate. She commanded over 70,000 pirates and 1,800 ships, and punished even the smallest crimes with death. When she fell in love with a man who was not interested in her, she kept him in a wooden cage on the deck!

GIRL OR BOY?

Mary Read was born in England in 1692. Disguised as a boy, she joined the Royal Navy and sailed to the Caribbean. On the way there, her ship was captured by the pirate Calico Jack Rackham. He invited Mary to join his ship, and she accepted.

TEAMING UP

Anne Bonny ran away from her home in Carolina, USA. She fell in love with Captain Jack Rackham, the pirate who had invited Mary Read to join his ship. Mary and Anne became life-long friends and enjoyed many years of successful pirating together.

SORRY, IVY — YOU FORGOT TO HIDE YOUR BUNCHES! NO GIRLS!

SINCE WE'RE REAL PIRATES, WE'D BETTER TRY TO FIND A TREASURE ISLAND!

OH, OH! THE KIDS SHOULDN'T HAVE LET 'ERBERT READ THE MAP!

WE'RE GOING IN CIRCLES! I'M GOING UP TO THE CROWS' NEST!

I SPY WITH MY LITTLE EYE . . .

. . . A TREASURE ISLAND FOR US TO PLUNDER!

CRAWK!
OK, CROWS! YOU CAN HAVE YOUR NEST BACK, NOW!

ROGUES'

Anyone could become a pirate. Dissatisfied sailors, people looking for adventure on the high seas and those seeking their fortune all signed up for a life of plunder and pillage. Throughout history there have been thousands of pirates.

BLACKBEARD

Blackbeard was born in England. He is one of the most famous pirates of all. His real name was Edward Teach but he was known by many names. He was very tall with a black waist-length beard and frizzy hair. His beard was braided and knotted with silk ribbons. When attacking another ship, he attached burning fuses to his hair to frighten away his opponents.

HENRY MORGAN

Under orders from Oliver Cromwell, Henry Morgan attacked Spanish ships and treasure ports. When it came to attacking the Spanish, Morgan enjoyed such amazing success that King Charles II made him a knight. He also became the governor of Jamaica. So who says that crime doesn't pay?

GALLERY

BARTHOLOMEW 'BLACK BART' ROBERTS

Black Bart was a Welshman who was captured by pirates. Rather than be their prisoner, he decided to become a pirate himself and before long, he was captain. Between 1718 and 1722, he captured more than 400 ships. He was very cruel to his prisoners, frequently whipping them and cutting their ears off.

'CALICO JACK'

This was John Rackham's nickname, because he always dressed in bright calico cotton. He was unusual because he allowed females to sail with him. Rackham recruited both Anne Bonny and Mary Read and both of them fell in love with him.

CAPTAIN KIDD

Captain Kidd was hired to hunt down pirates. When he saw how rich some of them were, he decided to join them! He is said to have buried treasure on Long Island in the United States. Even today, people still search for it.

CAPTAIN JACK'S PIRATE QUIZ 2

Okay, you lily-livered sea dogs, Captain Jack's back with another quiz!

1. What diseases did pirates tend to suffer from?
2. What bus crossed the ocean?
3. What were ships' biscuits called?
4. Why can't your head be 12 inches wide?
5. What name did pirates have for eggs?
6. What was 'keel-hauling'?
7. What did pirates like to drink, instead of water?

ANSWERS

1. Malaria, yellow fever and typhus. 2. Colum-bus. 3. Hard tack. 4. Because then it would be a foot. 5. 'Cackle fruit'. 6. A person tied to the back of a ship and dragged underneath. 7. Beer.

MEANWHILE —
AH! IT'S GREAT BEING THE KIDS' TEACHER WHEN YOU'RE MILES AWAY FROM THEM ON A DESERT ISLAND!
A RICH LANDLUBBER! ATTACK, PIRATES!
HAR! WE'VE GOT OURSELVES A REAL LIVE CAPTIVE!
HE'S GOT BICCIES!
UMFF!

HAVE YOU GOT WHAT IT TAKES TO BE A PIRATE?

The Secret Pirate Recruiting Service are running a recruitment drive. If you would like to be a pirate, answer the following questions. You need to get all the answers right in order to qualify.

1. Are you willing to be seen in public places 'wearing' the following?
   - Spotted scarf tied round your head
   - Two large gold earrings
   - A parrot (not worn exactly, but perched on your shoulder)
   - An eye patch
   - Extremely smelly baggy trousers
   - One wooden leg

   a) Yes, no problem there.

   b) No, you'll pass.

   c) You'd rather be flogged with a cat-o'-nine tails.

2. Can you jump out in front of adults, at every opportunity, (reducing them to shivering wrecks, because that's what skilled pirates do) and utter the following (in a loud booming voice) " 'and over all yer valuables, matey, or I'll sliver yer onions!"

   a) Yes, of course. You'll begin practising straight away.

   b) No. You'll pass again.

   c) You'd rather be abandoned on a desert island.

3. Can you drink gallons of your favourite soft drink and then sing the following pirate ballad very loudly, out of tune, all night long?

I live a life of danger
I'm hardly ever home.
The high seas are my manger
The oceans I do roam.

I might be slightly smelly,
With whiskers on my face.
My breath might smell like onions,
My manners out of place.

For I'm a nasty pirate,
Of me you should take fright.
For I can cook your gibblets
Sneak up on you at night.

Chorus
Ho ho, ha ha, he he,
smelly Jack(ie) that's me.

a) Yes. This is, in fact, your favourite ballad.
b) No. You'll have to pass yet again.
c) You'd rather eat worm-wriggling ship's biscuits for the next three years!

4. Are you dragged kicking and screaming to the bathroom when parents insist you have a bath or a shower?

a) Yes. The very sight of soap and water makes you break out in boils.
b) No. You actually quite like being clean.
c) Never. Because you never wash!

ANSWERS
1.a); 2.a); 3.a); 4.a) or c)

If you have scored full points, then you have passed the entrance test. You are indeed a yellow-livered, mean-dog of a pirate. Well done!

MY PIRATE SHIP NEEDS YOU!

NOW TO LOOK UPON THE FACE OF THIS CAPTIVE WHO EATS THE SAME BICCIES AS TEACHER!
ARGH! IT IS TEACHER!
DIDN'T TAKE YOU LOT LONG TO TURN TO PIRACY WITHOUT ME!
HARUMPH!
RUN FOR IT, KIDS!

STOP RIGHT THERE. THE CANNON'S LOADED WITH OLIVE'S DUMPLINGS!
WE SURRENDER!
TEACHER'S MAKING US WALK THE PLANK!
HAR! HAR!
INTO A VAT OF OLIVE'S CUSTARD! THIS IS WORSE THAN BEING THROWN TO THE SHARKS!
GLUBBLE!
BLURP!

NOW RETURN THAT SHIP TO WHERE YOU FOUND IT!
SPOILSPORT!
ON THE WAY HOME A STORM BLOWS UP —
HOW DO YOU STOP THIS THING?
FATTY OVERBOARD!
WE SLOWED OURSELVES DOWN BY USING A BOY AS A BUOY!